beautifully
broken

jesus every day

Devotional Guide

CANDACE | DaySpring

candacecbure.com | dayspring.com

WELCOME!

Brokenness is a tough subject, but every one of us has experienced heartache, despair, and hopelessness. Deep down, most of us feel like we aren't good enough. We can't imagine how God could ever forgive us or love us after all we've done.

Or maybe when you compare yourself to others, you feel like you *are* good enough. But compared to Jesus, we are all sinful, dirty, and completely broken and needy—even if we don't feel like we are. We all fall short of Jesus' perfection.

In this devotional, we'll read stories from the Bible about broken people in need of God's healing. We'll learn how God restores us because in His eyes, we are totally worth saving. We'll also consider how to respond to God's restoration and encourage others with our stories.

In Isaiah 61:3, God promises us "a crown of beauty instead of ashes, the oil of joy instead of mourning, and a garment of praise instead of a spirit of despair" (NIV). You don't have to stay broken, my friend. Beauty is just around the corner!

In this together, *Candace*

Before You Get Started on This Adventure

*H*ere's the deal. You're picking this book up and are either super excited to dig in or wondering if you really want to start this journey with me. I get it. Trust me, I do. And while I can tell you that this study can undoubtedly change your life, you may not be eager to jump in based on my enthusiasm alone. But would you do me a favor? Would you at least read through this first section before you put this book back on the shelf?

Before jumping into it, you might be wondering why the Bible is worth reading or what all the talk about being "saved" means. You may feel like you'll never measure up to God's standards—that there's no hope for you—so why even try? Or maybe you feel like you're doing just fine and life is actually pretty good, so why would you need to dig deep into God's Word?

Wherever you are in your spiritual journey, I want you to know you're not alone. In this first section, I've answered some questions people typically ask me about my Christian faith. I hope these answers will be helpful to you too.

Why should I read and study the Bible?

The world is full of all kinds of books that tell stories, teach concepts, inspire, and entertain. Heck, I've even written a few of them! Many books have influenced the world throughout history, but none compare with the Bible.

We all love a good story, right? While the Bible is full of history, wisdom, guidelines, and poetry, it's actually the epic story about all of creation and time from the beginning to the end. In the Bible, God is the ultimate storyteller—He shares His plan, His story, and His design for the world and for humanity.

The story begins with God creating His beloved humanity—Adam and Eve—in His image. But they destroyed their relationship with Him by choosing power instead of trusting in Him. Then the rest of the Bible—the greatest love story ever told—continues as God sets His plan in motion to bring His people back to Himself.

While there are other books that claim to be "holy," and even some that may contain useful ideas or wise words, no other book explains so clearly humanity's desperate need for rescue and how God Himself came to the rescue by sending His only Son, Jesus. No other book is so transformational because no other book shows us how much we are *loved* by our Creator.

What does it mean to be "saved"?

When followers of Jesus talk about being saved, we mean that Jesus rescued us from the ultimate consequence of sin—eternal separation from God—and our lives are no longer controlled by sin or filled with darkness, hopelessness, shame, guilt, and fear.

Jesus shines His light, freedom, joy, peace, and hope into our lives. God doesn't want sin to have any control over us. He wants to have a relationship with us. He wants us to live full, abundant, joyful lives that reflect His goodness back to others! That's why Jesus came—to save us from the punishment we deserve because of our sin and to give us new life.

Being saved doesn't mean we are spared from all suffering in our lives. But it does mean we have God's presence with us and the promise of spending forever with Him—an eternity free from all pain and suffering. Jesus is ready to save us the moment we open our hearts to Him and accept His unconditional love for us.

What if I don't need to be "saved"?

I get this too—you're a good person, you help others, you live honestly, you probably donate time and money to charity, and you're not hurting anyone. Why do you need to be "saved"? Compared to others, you're practically a saint! But God's standards are different from human standards. If we just compare ourselves to other people, it's easy to think we're good enough. But when we compare ourselves to God's standards, we fall miserably short. Every. Single. Time.

We all deserve God's judgment. Because He is holy, He cannot allow sin anywhere near Him. Because of sin, we cannot earn our way to having a relationship with God. Our sin separates us from our Creator. God says that if we break even one commandment, it's as if we're guilty of breaking them all. There isn't one of us who can say we are sinless. And doing good things to earn God's approval doesn't erase our sinfulness either. But because God loves us, He sent His Son, Jesus, to die so that all people—the bad, the good, and everyone in between—could have a relationship with Him.

ecause I believe the Bible shows us who Jesus is and how we can have a relationship with Him, I want to help you get to know Him too. That's what this study guide is all about.

How do I use this study guide?

Here's how it works: each day has a reading from the Bible and then some questions to help you think about and apply the biblical concepts. It's that simple! There's no "right" answer, and you can add your own questions and thoughts at any point, on any page.

Ideally, this is a personal journey where God will speak directly to your heart. But going through the study with friends can bring you encouragement and help you connect with others in really valuable ways. If you'd like, you could complete a day's study alone and then come together with a group of friends to discuss what God is showing you. You decide!

Let's do this!

As you go through each day's study, pray through it. Don't just complete it so you can check it off your to-do list. And don't look to me to tell you the answers or what to think; look to the Word and ask God to speak to you. Lastly, don't be afraid. The most repeated command in the Bible is "Do not fear," and one of the most common promises from God is "I am with you." So jump into this adventure and ask God what He wants to reveal to you.

Whether you are new to the Bible or super familiar with it, I can tell you this: God's Word is living and active. It will bring you life, and you will thrive every day as you find truth, peace, and hope within its pages. Let's go!

Adam and Eve:
Broken and Ashamed

Genesis 3:1–8, 20–21 (NIV)

Now the serpent was more crafty than any of the wild animals the Lord God had made. He said to the woman, "Did God really say, 'You must not eat from any tree in the garden'?"

The woman said to the serpent, "We may eat fruit from the trees in the garden, but God did say, 'You must not eat fruit from the tree that is in the middle of the garden, and you must not touch it, or you will die.' "

"You will not certainly die," the serpent said to the woman. "For God knows that when you eat from it your eyes will be opened, and you will be like God, knowing good and evil." When the woman saw that the fruit of the tree was good for food and pleasing to the eye, and also desirable for gaining wisdom, she took some and ate it. She also gave some to her husband, who was with her, and he ate it. Then the eyes of both of them were opened, and they realized they were naked; so they sewed fig leaves together and made coverings for themselves. Then the man and his wife heard the sound of the Lord God as He was walking in the garden in the cool of the day, and they hid from the Lord God among the trees of the garden. . . .

Adam named his wife Eve, because she would become the mother of all the living. The Lord God made garments of skin for Adam and his wife and clothed them.

*For more on Adam and Eve's story, read Genesis 2:18–25; 3:11–4:26.

What is your understanding of what it means to sin?

Adam and Eve were ashamed and hid from God after they disobeyed

Him. How do you tend to act when you rebel against God?

How did God show His love and care for Adam and Eve even after they had sinned against Him?

GOD

WILL NOT ABANDON

YOU.

In what ways has God shown His love for you even after you have rebelled against Him?

_____

_____

_____

_____

_____

_____

_____

_____

_____

_____

_____

_____

A NOTE FROM CANDACE

Maybe you really messed up. Maybe you hurt someone or feel like God has abandoned you. Maybe you feel unbearably broken or disappointed . . . but dare to hope again—ask God to reveal His love to you and show you what you can learn from this difficult experience.

DAY 2

Moses:
Broken
and Insecure

EXODUS 3:10–12; 4:10–17 (NLT)

[God said,] "Now go, for I am sending you to Pharaoh. You must lead My people Israel out of Egypt."

But Moses protested to God, "Who am I to appear before Pharaoh? Who am I to lead the people of Israel out of Egypt?"

God answered, "I will be with you." . . .

But Moses pleaded with the LORD, "O Lord, I'm not very good with words. I never have been, and I'm not now, even though You have spoken to me. I get tongue-tied, and my words get tangled."

Then the LORD asked Moses, "Who makes a person's mouth? Who decides whether people speak or do not speak, hear or do not hear, see or do not see? Is it not I, the LORD? Now go! I will be with you as you speak, and I will instruct you in what to say."

But Moses again pleaded, "Lord, please! Send anyone else."

Then the LORD became angry with Moses. "All right," He said. "What about your brother, Aaron the Levite? . . . He will be your mouthpiece, and you will stand in the place of God for him, telling him what to say. And take your shepherd's staff with you, and use it to perform the miraculous signs I have shown you."

*For more on Moses' story, read Exodus 2:1–14:31; Numbers 20:1–13.

When have you been given a task you felt was too difficult to accomplish? What happened?

Based on what you've read in the verses from Exodus, how did Moses view himself? How does that compare with how you view yourself?

Moses' insecurity didn't stop God from wanting Moses to serve Him. How did God meet Moses' needs in these verses?

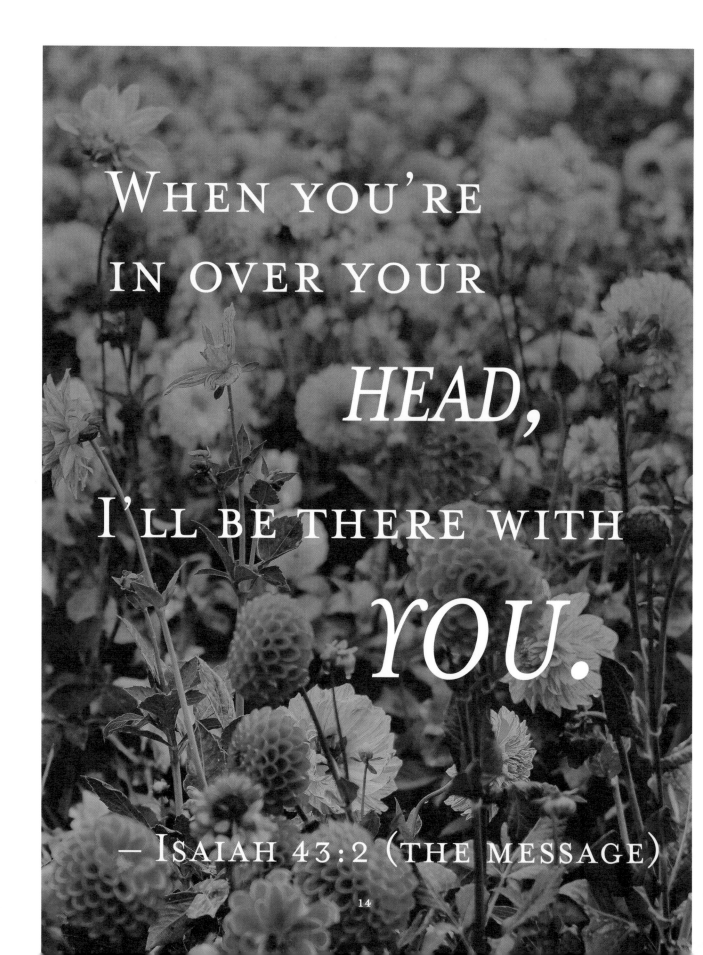

WHEN YOU'RE IN OVER YOUR

HEAD,

I'LL BE THERE WITH

YOU.

— ISAIAH 43:2 (THE MESSAGE)

God gave Moses a huge job and then told him, "I will be with you." How do those words encourage you today?

_____

_____

_____

_____

_____

_____

_____

_____

_____

_____

_____

_____

_____

YOUR BIGGEST TAKEAWAY

15

Hannah:
Broken and Sorrowful

I Samuel 1:1–20 (CSB)

There was a man from Ramathaim-zophim in the hill country of Ephraim. . . . He had two wives, the first named Hannah and the second Peninnah. Peninnah had children, but Hannah was childless. . . . Deeply hurt, Hannah prayed to the LORD and wept with many tears. Making a vow, she pleaded, "LORD of Armies, if You will take notice of your servant's affliction, remember and not forget me, and give Your servant a son, I will give him to the LORD all the days of his life, and his hair will never be cut."

While she continued praying in the LORD's presence, Eli watched her mouth. Hannah was praying silently, and though her lips were moving, her voice could not be heard. Eli thought she was drunk and said to her, "How long are you going to be drunk? Get rid of your wine!"

"No, my lord," Hannah replied. "I am a woman with a broken heart. I haven't had any wine or beer; I've been pouring out my heart before the LORD. Don't think of me as a wicked woman; I've been praying from the depth of my anguish and resentment."

Eli responded, "Go in peace, and may the God of Israel grant the request you've made of Him." . . . After some time, Hannah conceived and gave birth to a son. She named him Samuel, because she said, "I requested him from the LORD."

*For more on Hannah's story, read I Samuel 1:1–2:21.

What experiences in your life have caused you deep sorrow or feelings of hopelessness?

Hannah took her heartbreak to God in prayer. How would

you describe Hannah's prayer in these verses?

In what ways can you identify with Hannah's experience?

IF YOU *BELIEVE* IN PRAYER AT ALL, EXPECT *GOD* TO HEAR YOU.

— CHARLES SPURGEON

What currently causes you anguish, pain, or resentment? If you'd like, write

a prayer, asking God to heal your pain and provide you with hope.

_____

_____

_____

_____

_____

_____

_____

_____

_____

_____

_____

_____

_____

_____

_____

YOUR BIGGEST TAKEAWAY

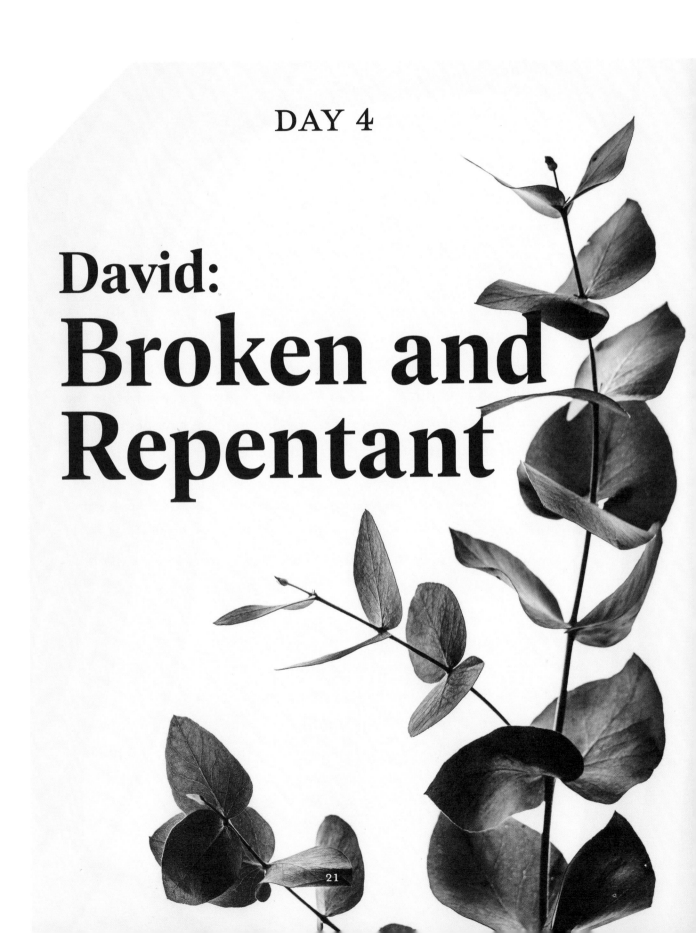

David:
Broken and Repentant

II Samuel 12:7–18 (ESV)

|

Nathan said to David, "You are the man! Thus says the LORD, the God of Israel, 'I anointed you king over Israel, and I delivered you out of the hand of Saul. And I gave you your master's house and your master's wives into your arms and gave you the house of Israel and of Judah. And if this were too little, I would add to you as much more. Why have you despised the word of the LORD, to do what is evil in his sight? You have struck down Uriah the Hittite with the sword and have taken his wife to be your wife and have killed him with the sword of the Ammonites. Now therefore the sword shall never depart from your house, because you have despised me and have taken the wife of Uriah the Hittite to be your wife.' " . . .

David said to Nathan, "I have sinned against the LORD." And Nathan said to David, "The LORD also has put away your sin; you shall not die. Nevertheless, because by this deed you have utterly scorned the LORD, the child who is born to you shall die." Then Nathan went to his house.

And the LORD afflicted the child that Uriah's wife bore to David, and he became sick. David therefore sought God on behalf of the child. And David fasted and went in and lay all night on the ground. And the elders of his house stood beside him, to raise him from the ground, but he would not, nor did he eat food with them. On the seventh day the child died.

*For more on David's story, read II Samuel 11:1–12:25.

When in your life have you had to face negative consequences for your actions?

In these verses, King David is confronted by a prophet named Nathan about his sinful actions—adultery and murder. How does David respond to Nathan's message from God?

Even though David repented of his sin, what consequences did he have to face? Who did those consequences affect besides David?

REPENTANCE

LEADS TO

FORGIVENESS.

What can you learn from David's experience of brokenness because

of his sin and the forgiveness he received from God?

_____

_____

_____

_____

_____

_____

_____

_____

_____

_____

_____

_____

_____

_____

_____

A NOTE FROM CANDACE

In my teenage years, I thought I was a good person. I went to church and even read the Bible once in a while. But in my early 20s I realized that God is going to judge me by *His* standards, and I was breaking His laws. The good news is that Jesus paid my fine. Because I'm grateful to Him, I acknowledge my sin and repent of it.

A Sick Woman:
Broken and Healed

MARK 5:25—34 (NIV)

And a woman was there who had been subject to bleeding for twelve years. She had suffered a great deal under the care of many doctors and had spent all she had, yet instead of getting better she grew worse. When she heard about Jesus, she came up behind Him in the crowd and touched His cloak, because she thought, "If I just touch His clothes, I will be healed." Immediately her bleeding stopped and she felt in her body that she was freed from her suffering.

At once Jesus realized that power had gone out from Him. He turned around in the crowd and asked, "Who touched My clothes?"

"You see the people crowding against You," His disciples answered, "and yet You can ask, 'Who touched Me?' "

But Jesus kept looking around to see who had done it. Then the woman, knowing what had happened to her, came and fell at His feet and, trembling with fear, told Him the whole truth. He said to her, "Daughter, your faith has healed you. Go in peace and be freed from your suffering."

*For more on the sick woman's story, read Matthew 9:20—22; Luke 8:42—48.

When have you cried out to God to heal your physical or emotional brokenness?

How does this story of healing demonstrate Jesus' power to heal?

How would you describe the woman's faith in Jesus? How does her faith compare to your own faith?

HEAL ME,
LORD,
AND I WILL BE
HEALED.

– JEREMIAH 17:14 (NIV)

Describe your belief or lack of faith in Jesus' power to save you, forgive you,

restore you, and heal you. In what ways do you need to trust Him more?

YOUR BIGGEST TAKEAWAY

Peter:
Broken and Remorseful

MATTHEW 26:57–58, 69–75 (NLT)

Then the people who had arrested Jesus led Him to the home of Caiaphas, the high priest, where the teachers of religious law and the elders had gathered. Meanwhile, Peter followed Him at a distance and came to the high priest's courtyard. . . . A servant girl came over and said to him, "You were one of those with Jesus the Galilean."

But Peter denied it in front of everyone. "I don't know what you're talking about," he said.

Later, out by the gate, another servant girl noticed him and said to those standing around, "This man was with Jesus of Nazareth."

Again Peter denied it, this time with an oath. "I don't even know the man," he said.

A little later some of the other bystanders came over to Peter and said, "You must be one of them; we can tell by your Galilean accent."

Peter swore, "A curse on me if I'm lying—I don't know the man!" And immediately the rooster crowed. Suddenly, Jesus' words flashed through Peter's mind: "Before the rooster crows, you will deny three times that you even know Me." And he went away, weeping bitterly.

*For more on Peter's story, read Matthew 26:31–56; John 21:1–19.

Have you ever been betrayed by a close friend? How did that betrayal affect your relationship?

Why do you think Peter, who had been one of Jesus' disciples and closest friends, denied knowing Jesus? In what ways can you relate to Peter in this situation?

What does Peter's response to hearing the rooster crow reveal about his feelings about his actions and about his heart toward Jesus?

THE VOICE OF SIN IS *LOUD,*

BUT THE VOICE OF FORGIVENESS IS *LOUDER.*

— Dwight L. Moody

The relationship between Peter and Jesus was eventually restored (see John 21). What relationships in your life need forgiveness and restoration? What steps can you take this week to seek healing in those relationships?

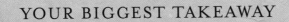

YOUR BIGGEST TAKEAWAY

The Lost Son:
Broken and Restored

LUKE 15:11—24 (HCSB)

[Jesus] said: "A man had two sons. The younger of them said to his father, 'Father, give me the share of the estate I have coming to me.' So he distributed the assets to them. Not many days later, the younger son gathered together all he had and traveled to a distant country, where he squandered his estate in foolish living. After he had spent everything, a severe famine struck that country, and he had nothing. Then he went to work for one of the citizens of that country, who sent him into his fields to feed pigs. He longed to eat his fill from the carob pods the pigs were eating, but no one would give him any. When he came to his senses, he said, 'How many of my father's hired hands have more than enough food, and here I am dying of hunger! I'll get up, go to my father, and say to him, Father, I have sinned against heaven and in your sight. I'm no longer worthy to be called your son. Make me like one of your hired hands.' So he got up and went to his father. But while the son was still a long way off, his father saw him and was filled with compassion. He ran, threw his arms around his neck, and kissed him. The son said to him, 'Father, I have sinned against heaven and in your sight. I'm no longer worthy to be called your son.' But the father told his slaves, 'Quick! Bring out the best robe and put it on him; put a ring on his finger and sandals on his feet. Then bring the fattened calf and slaughter it, and let's celebrate with a feast, because this son of mine was dead and is alive again; he was lost and is found!' So they began to celebrate."

*For more on the lost son's story, read Luke 15:25—32.

What words would you use to describe God as a Father?

In what ways do you identify with the lost son in the parable? Why?

What is surprising to you about the father's words or actions in the story? How do the father's words and actions compare to how God speaks and acts toward sinful humans?

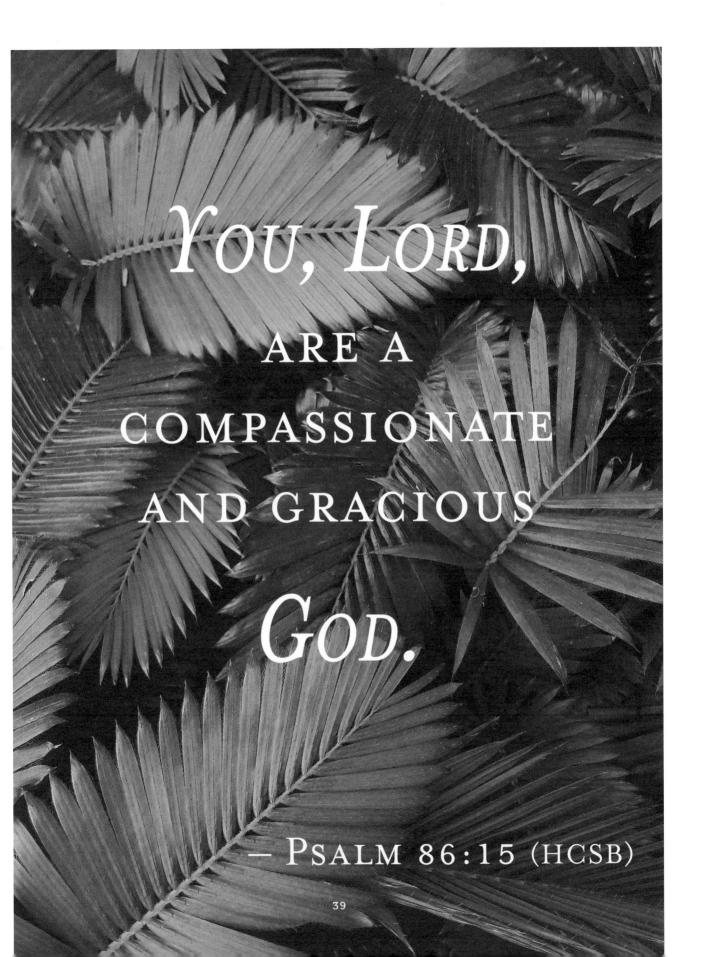

YOU, LORD, ARE A COMPASSIONATE AND GRACIOUS GOD.

— PSALM 86:15 (HCSB)

Use this space to write a prayer to God, the Father, thanking Him for loving you as you are—even in your rebelliousness and brokenness—and asking Him to forgive you for your sinful thoughts and actions.

_____

_____

_____

_____

_____

_____

_____

_____

_____

_____

_____

_____

A NOTE FROM CANDACE

Putting the pieces of your broken life back together takes work. No matter what you did, no matter who let you down, you can always run to Him. This doesn't mean life will immediately be easy. But Jesus sees our rawness, brokenness, and fear. And He loves us anyway. We don't have to face it alone.

Criminal on the Cross: Broken and Delivered

LUKE 23:24, 32–43 (NLT)

So Pilate sentenced Jesus to die as they demanded. . . . Two others, both criminals, were led out to be executed with Him. When they came to a place called The Skull, they nailed Him to the cross. And the criminals were also crucified—one on His right and one on His left. Jesus said, "Father, forgive them, for they don't know what they are doing." And the soldiers gambled for His clothes by throwing dice.

The crowd watched and the leaders scoffed. "He saved others," they said, "let Him save Himself if He is really God's Messiah, the Chosen One." The soldiers mocked Him, too, by offering Him a drink of sour wine. They called out to Him, "If You are the King of the Jews, save Yourself!" A sign was fastened above Him with these words: "This is the King of the Jews."

One of the criminals hanging beside Him scoffed, "So You're the Messiah, are You? Prove it by saving Yourself—and us, too, while You're at it!"

But the other criminal protested, "Don't you fear God even when you have been sentenced to die? We deserve to die for our crimes, but this man hasn't done anything wrong." Then he said, "Jesus, remember me when You come into Your Kingdom."

And Jesus replied, "I assure you, today you will be with Me in paradise."

*For more on the criminal's story, read Matthew 27:38–44; Mark 15:27–32.

What do you believe about Jesus—who He is and what He has done for you?

How do the two criminals crucified next to Jesus differ in how they viewed Jesus?

Even though he was hanging on a cross as punishment for his crimes, what did the second criminal receive as a result of his faith in Jesus?

FOR THE WAGES OF SIN IS DEATH, BUT THE FREE GIFT OF GOD IS ETERNAL

LIFE

THROUGH CHRIST JESUS OUR LORD.

— ROMANS 6:23 (NLT)

Just like the criminals crucified next to Jesus, we deserve to be punished for our sins. But God sent Jesus to save us from the ultimate consequence of sins—eternal separation from God. He gives us the gift of eternal life with Him when we trust in Jesus to save us. Take a moment to write down your response to God's gift of eternal life to you through Jesus.

YOUR BIGGEST TAKEAWAY

The Apostle Paul:
Broken and Transformed

I TIMOTHY 1:12–17 (TLB)

How thankful I am to Christ Jesus our Lord for choosing me as one of His messengers, and giving me the strength to be faithful to Him, even though I used to scoff at the name of Christ. I hunted down His people, harming them in every way I could. But God had mercy on me because I didn't know what I was doing, for I didn't know Christ at that time. Oh, how kind our Lord was, for He showed me how to trust Him and become full of the love of Christ Jesus.

How true it is, and how I long that everyone should know it, that Christ Jesus came into the world to save sinners—and I was the greatest of them all. But God had mercy on me so that Christ Jesus could use me as an example to show everyone how patient He is with even the worst sinners, so that others will realize that they, too, can have everlasting life. Glory and honor to God forever and ever. He is the King of the ages, the unseen One who never dies; He alone is God, and full of wisdom. Amen.

*For more on the apostle Paul's story, read Acts 9:1–31; 13:1–12.

How would you describe what it means to show mercy to someone?

Based on these verses, what kind of person was the apostle Paul before he knew and loved Jesus? In what ways did Paul change after meeting Jesus?

According to these verses, how and why did God demonstrate mercy toward the apostle Paul?

CHRIST JESUS CAME INTO THE WORLD TO SAVE SINNERS.

Describe your life before and after meeting Jesus. If you've placed your trust in Him as your Savior, how have you experienced God's mercy in your life?

YOUR BIGGEST TAKEAWAY

God's Merciful Forgiveness

MICAH 7:7—9, 18—20 (NIV)

Because I have sinned against Him,
   I will bear the LORD's wrath,
until He pleads my case
   and upholds my cause.
He will bring me out into the light;
   I will see His righteousness. . . .

Who is a God like You,
   who pardons sin and forgives the transgression
   of the remnant of His inheritance?
You do not stay angry forever
   but delight to show mercy.
You will again have compassion on us;
   You will tread our sins underfoot
   and hurl all our iniquities into the depths of the sea.
You will be faithful to Jacob,
   and show love to Abraham,
as You pledged on oath to our ancestors
   in days long ago.

How have you experienced discipline—facing the consequences of your poor decisions—in your life? How have you grown from those experiences?

What comfort can you find in these verses for times when you are broken, when you mess up and sin?

According to these verses, how does God show His faithfulness and love to His people?

GOD DELIGHTS TO SHOW MERCY.

What hope do you have for your future as a result of God's forgiveness of your sin?

In what ways can you share that hope with other people this week?

A NOTE FROM CANDACE

Compared to Jesus, we'll never measure up. He lived a sinless life. But the amazing thing is He knows we've messed up and that we'll mess up again, yet He loves us unconditionally and died for us anyway! He didn't leave us to sit in our brokenness—He came to save us, forgive us, and restore our relationship with Him.

Healing for the Brokenhearted

PSALMS 34:18—22; 147:1—7 (TLB)

The Lord is close to those whose hearts are breaking; He rescues those who are humbly sorry for their sins. The good man does not escape all troubles—he has them too. But the Lord helps him in each and every one. Not one of his bones is broken.

Calamity will surely overtake the wicked; heavy penalties are meted out to those who hate the good. But as for those who serve the Lord, He will redeem them; everyone who takes refuge in Him will be freely pardoned.

Hallelujah! Yes, praise the Lord! How good it is to sing His praises! How delightful, and how right!

He is rebuilding Jerusalem and bringing back the exiles. He heals the brokenhearted, binding up their wounds. He counts the stars and calls them all by name. How great He is! His power is absolute! His understanding is unlimited. The Lord supports the humble, but brings the wicked into the dust.

Sing out your thanks to Him; sing praises to our God, accompanied by harps.

Describe a time when your heart was breaking. Who helped you through that situation?

The Bible doesn't promise anyone a life free of problems. But according to these verses,
how does God help His people through times of heartbreak or trouble?

How does the author of Psalm 147 respond to God's healing of the brokenhearted?
How does that response compare to how you tend to respond to God's healing in your life?

GOD

HEALS

BROKEN

HEARTS.

In these verses we read that God "rescues those who are humbly sorry for their sins."

How often do you humble yourself and ask God for His forgiveness?

If you'd like, write down a prayer here, asking God to forgive you and to heal you.

_____

_____

_____

_____

_____

_____

_____

_____

_____

_____

_____

_____

YOUR BIGGEST TAKEAWAY

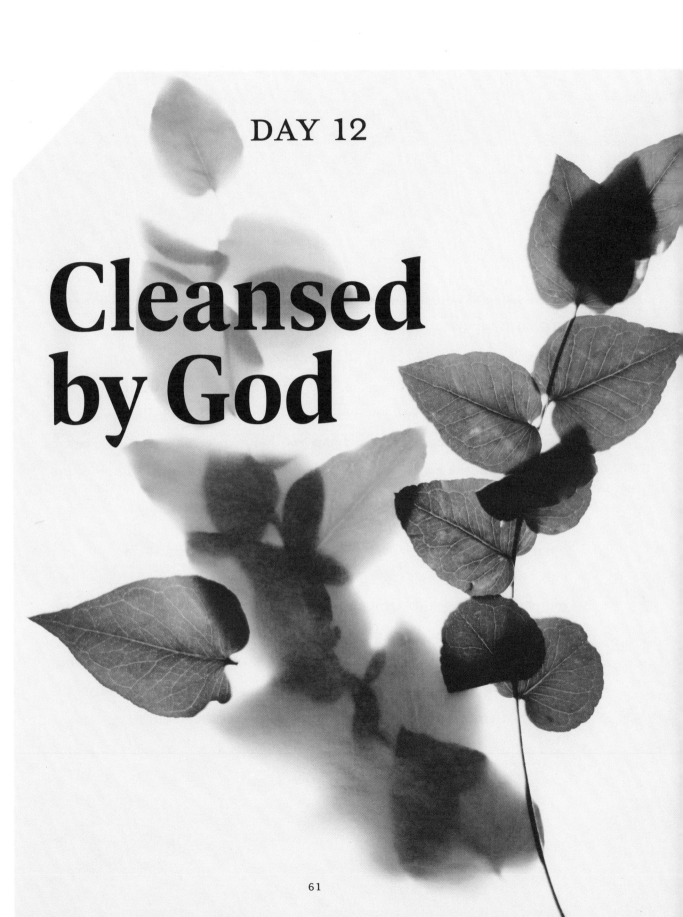

Cleansed by God

PSALM 51:1–12 (TLB)

O loving and kind God, have mercy. Have pity upon me and take away the awful stain of my transgressions. Oh, wash me, cleanse me from this guilt. Let me be pure again. For I admit my shameful deed—it haunts me day and night. It is against You and You alone I sinned and did this terrible thing. You saw it all, and your sentence against me is just. But I was born a sinner, yes, from the moment my mother conceived me. You deserve honesty from the heart; yes, utter sincerity and truthfulness. Oh, give me this wisdom.

Sprinkle me with the cleansing blood and I shall be clean again. Wash me and I shall be whiter than snow. And after You have punished me, give me back my joy again. Don't keep looking at my sins—erase them from Your sight. Create in me a new, clean heart, O God, filled with clean thoughts and right desires. Don't toss me aside, banished forever from Your presence. Don't take Your Holy Spirit from me. Restore to me again the joy of Your salvation, and make me willing to obey You.

When have you recently prayed to God and asked Him to forgive you?

These verses were written by King David as a prayer of repentance after he committed both adultery and murder. In what ways do you relate to David's feelings and desires in his prayer?

What can you learn from these verses about the character of God?

What can you learn about David's relationship with God?

CREATE IN ME
A NEW,

CLEAN

HEART,

O GOD.

In what areas of your life do you need to be washed clean? In what areas of your life are you lacking joy? Write down a prayer, asking God to cleanse you and restore joy in your life.

_____

_____

_____

_____

_____

_____

_____

_____

_____

_____

_____

_____

_____

YOUR BIGGEST TAKEAWAY

DAY 13

Restored by God

JEREMIAH 33:1—11 (CSB)

While he was still confined in the guard's courtyard, the word of the LORD came to Jeremiah a second time: "The LORD who made the earth, the LORD who forms it to establish it, the LORD is His name, says this: Call to Me and I will answer you and tell you great and incomprehensible things you do not know. . . . I will restore the fortunes of Judah and of Israel and will rebuild them as in former times. I will purify them from all the iniquity they have committed against Me, and I will forgive all the iniquities they have committed against Me, rebelling against Me. This city will bear on My behalf a name of joy, praise, and glory before all the nations of the earth, who will hear of all the prosperity I will give them. They will tremble with awe because of all the good and all the peace I will bring about for them.

"This is what the LORD says: In this place, which you say is a ruin, without people or animals—that is, in Judah's cities and Jerusalem's streets that are a desolation without people, without inhabitants, and without animals—there will be heard again a sound of joy and gladness, the voice of the groom and the bride, and the voice of those saying,

> Give thanks to the LORD of Armies,
> for the LORD is good;
> His faithful love endures forever

as they bring thank offerings to the temple of the LORD. For I will restore the fortunes of the land as in former times, says the LORD."

In what areas of your life do you currently feel broken or hopeless?

The prophet Jeremiah warned the people of Judah that they would be taken into captivity by the Babylonians because they turned their backs on God. But Jeremiah also reassured them of God's forgiveness and His promises. In these verses, what promises does God make to the people of Judah?

What do you learn about God and His character in these verses?

RESTORE US, *GOD;*

MAKE YOUR FACE *SHINE ON US,*

SO THAT WE MAY BE *SAVED.*

— PSALM 80:3 (CSB)

How has God healed and restored you? Take some time to joyfully respond to His

goodness to you by writing down all the ways He has healed and restored you.

A NOTE FROM CANDACE

I used to feel self-conscious about my high-pitched, "squeaky" voice. But recently I started reading Scriptures out loud on social media, and guess what? People seem to love it! Some have even commented, "I could listen to you all day long." Isn't this just like Jesus? What the world hates, He redeems. Incredible, right?

DAY 14

Fully Free

ROMANS 6:17–23; II CORINTHIANS 3:17; GALATIANS 5:1 (NIV)

But thanks be to God that, though you used to be slaves to sin, you have come to obey from your heart the pattern of teaching that has now claimed your allegiance. You have been set free from sin and have become slaves to righteousness.

I am using an example from everyday life because of your human limitations. Just as you used to offer yourselves as slaves to impurity and to ever-increasing wickedness, so now offer yourselves as slaves to righteousness leading to holiness. When you were slaves to sin, you were free from the control of righteousness. What benefit did you reap at that time from the things you are now ashamed of? Those things result in death! But now that you have been set free from sin and have become slaves of God, the benefit you reap leads to holiness, and the result is eternal life. For the wages of sin is death, but the gift of God is eternal life in Christ Jesus our Lord.

Now the Lord is the Spirit, and where the Spirit of the Lord is, there is freedom.

It is for freedom that Christ has set us free. Stand firm, then, and do not let yourselves be burdened again by a yoke of slavery.

Have you ever felt trapped or enslaved—perhaps in an unhealthy relationship, by a bad habit or attitude, or in a negative job situation? How did you feel when you were set free?

Based on these verses, what do you think it means for followers of Jesus to be "slaves to righteousness" or "slaves of God"?

According to these verses, what are the consequences of being slaves to sin? What are the benefits of being slaves of God?

WHERE THE *SPIRIT* OF THE *LORD IS,* THERE IS *FREEDOM.*

How have you experienced God's freedom in your life? In what ways can

you share the good news of that freedom with others this week?

YOUR BIGGEST TAKEAWAY

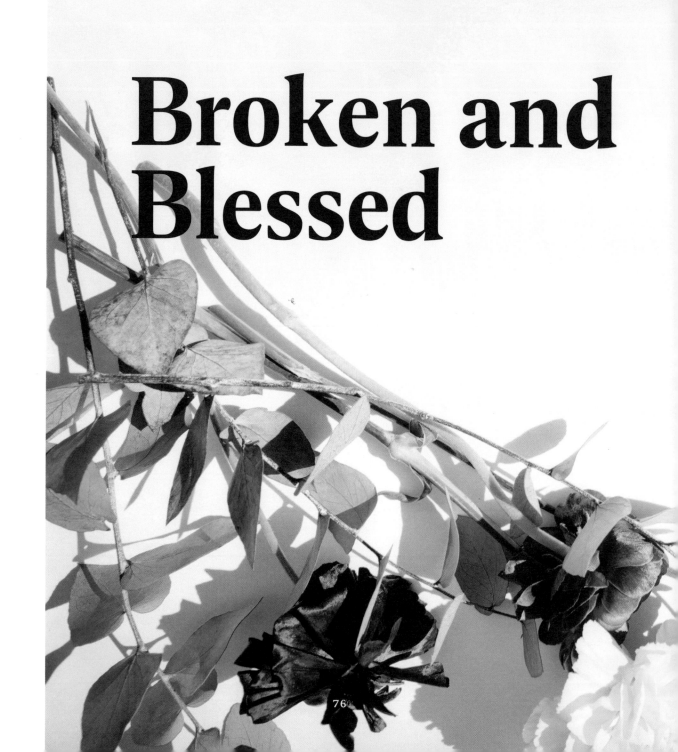

Broken and Blessed

MATTHEW 5:3–10 (NLT)

"God blesses those who are poor and realize their need for Him,

    for the Kingdom of Heaven is theirs.

God blesses those who mourn,

    for they will be comforted.

God blesses those who are humble,

    for they will inherit the whole earth.

God blesses those who hunger and thirst for justice,

    for they will be satisfied.

God blesses those who are merciful,

    for they will be shown mercy.

God blesses those whose hearts are pure,

    for they will see God.

God blesses those who work for peace,

    for they will be called the children of God.

God blesses those who are persecuted for doing right,

    for the Kingdom of Heaven is theirs."

When you hear the word "blessing," what comes to mind?

How have you been blessed in the past year?

In these verses from Matthew, what are the blessings that God gives people?

Which recipients of God's blessings in these verses do you most identify with? Why?

GOD

HAS SHOWERED

YOU WITH

BLESSINGS.

— PSALM 116:7 (THE MESSAGE)

Consider the broken people God blesses in Matthew 5:3–10. What are some

practical ways you can reach out to help people who are mourning or hungry

or who need justice? How else can you apply these verses to your life?

_____

_____

_____

_____

_____

_____

_____

_____

_____

_____

_____

_____

_____

YOUR BIGGEST TAKEAWAY

Strength Renewed

Isaiah 40:25–31 (NLT)

"To whom will you compare Me?

Who is My equal?" asks the Holy One.

Look up into the heavens.

Who created all the stars? . . .

Because of His great power and incomparable strength,

not a single one is missing. . . .

Have you never heard?

Have you never understood?

The Lord is the everlasting God,

the Creator of all the earth.

He never grows weak or weary.

No one can measure the depths of His understanding.

He gives power to the weak

and strength to the powerless.

Even youths will become weak and tired,

and young men will fall in exhaustion.

But those who trust in the Lord will find new strength.

They will soar high on wings like eagles.

They will run and not grow weary.

They will walk and not faint.

How has trusting in God for strength helped you in specific circumstances in your life?

How do these verses encourage you in what you're experiencing in your life right now?

What characteristics of God are mentioned in these verses? What promises of God are given?

HE GIVES POWER TO THE *WEAK* AND STRENGTH TO THE *POWERLESS.*

How can you encourage someone this week with

God's promises from these verses in Isaiah?

A NOTE FROM CANDACE

Embrace God as your source of strength and hope, and trust Him to bring you through seasons of brokenness. It's important to me that my children see me lean on God because I want them to know what to do when life gets difficult for them. Let others see God's strength in you so they'll understand that He can strengthen them too.

DAY 17

Encouraging Others

I Thessalonians 5:2–11 (NLT)

You know quite well that the day of the Lord's return will come unexpectedly, like a thief in the night. When people are saying, "Everything is peaceful and secure," then disaster will fall on them as suddenly as a pregnant woman's labor pains begin. And there will be no escape.

But you aren't in the dark about these things, dear brothers and sisters, and you won't be surprised when the day of the Lord comes like a thief. For you are all children of the light and of the day; we don't belong to darkness and night. So be on your guard, not asleep like the others. Stay alert and be clearheaded. Night is the time when people sleep and drinkers get drunk. But let us who live in the light be clearheaded, protected by the armor of faith and love, and wearing as our helmet the confidence of our salvation.

For God chose to save us through our Lord Jesus Christ, not to pour out His anger on us. Christ died for us so that, whether we are dead or alive when He returns, we can live with Him forever. So encourage each other and build each other up, just as you are already doing.

How do you feel about spending eternity with God? How are

you preparing your heart for Jesus' return?

According to these verses, how are followers of Jesus expected to live as we anticipate His return?

Based on what you read in the verses from I Thessalonians, why did Christ die

for us? What is your response to God sending His Son to save you?

ENCOURAGE EACH *OTHER* AND BUILD EACH *OTHER UP.*

The apostle Paul wrote, "So encourage each other and build each other up." How are you encouraging others? What can you do this week to encourage people in their faith?

YOUR BIGGEST TAKEAWAY

Devoted to What Is Good

TITUS 3:1–8 (CSB)

Remind them to submit to rulers and authorities, to obey, to be ready for every good work, to slander no one, to avoid fighting, and to be kind, always showing gentleness to all people. For we too were once foolish, disobedient, deceived, enslaved by various passions and pleasures, living in malice and envy, hateful, detesting one another.

But when the kindness of God our Savior and His love for mankind appeared, He saved us—not by works of righteousness that we had done, but according to His mercy—through the washing of regeneration and renewal by the Holy Spirit. He poured out His Spirit on us abundantly through Jesus Christ our Savior so that, having been justified by His grace, we may become heirs with the hope of eternal life. This saying is trustworthy. I want you to insist on these things, so that those who have believed God might be careful to devote themselves to good works. These are good and profitable for everyone.

How do you respond to God's goodness in your life and to the forgiveness He offers you?

According to these verses, how has God shown kindness toward us?

Based on Titus 3:1—8, how should followers of Jesus live

in response to God's kindness in their lives?

BE READY FOR EVERY GOOD WORK.

Believers in God are called to "devote themselves to good works"—not in order to obtain salvation but in order to share God's love with others. What "good works" are you devoted to? What is your motivation for doing those things?

YOUR BIGGEST TAKEAWAY

Living Beautifully Broken

II Corinthians 4:8–18 (HCSB)

We are pressured in every way but not crushed; we are perplexed but not in despair; we are persecuted but not abandoned; we are struck down but not destroyed. We always carry the death of Jesus in our body, so that the life of Jesus may also be revealed in our body. For we who live are always given over to death because of Jesus, so that Jesus' life may also be revealed in our mortal flesh. So death works in us, but life in you. And since we have the same spirit of faith in keeping with what is written, I believed, therefore I spoke, we also believe, and therefore speak. We know that the One who raised the Lord Jesus will raise us also with Jesus and present us with you. Indeed, everything is for your benefit, so that grace, extended through more and more people, may cause thanksgiving to increase to God's glory.

Therefore we do not give up. Even though our outer person is being destroyed, our inner person is being renewed day by day. For our momentary light affliction is producing for us an absolutely incomparable eternal weight of glory. So we do not focus on what is seen, but on what is unseen. For what is seen is temporary, but what is unseen is eternal.

How easy is it for you to become discouraged or feel like giving

up when you face trying circumstances in your life?

According to II Corinthians 4:8–9, people who have received salvation through Jesus are "not crushed," "not in despair," "not abandoned," and "not destroyed" in the midst of their suffering. What encouragement for your life do you find in these verses?

What do you think the apostle Paul meant by the words "we do

not focus on what is seen, but on what is unseen"?

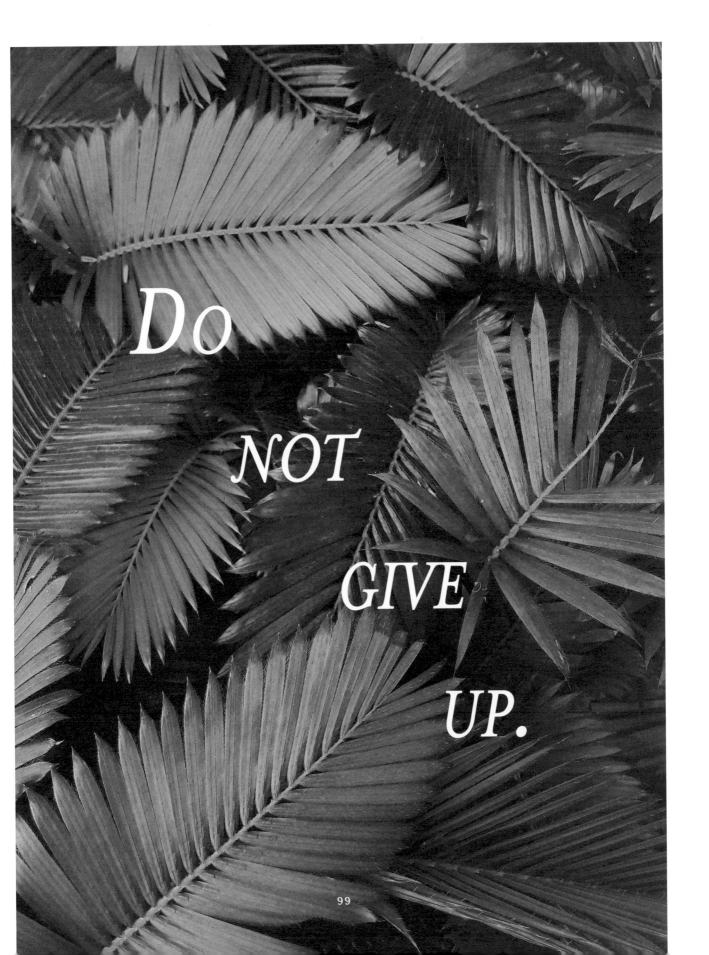

DO

NOT

GIVE

UP.

How has God used times of suffering in your life for your benefit? How might He be using the struggles you are currently facing to help you understand more of His grace in your life?

_____

_____

_____

_____

_____

_____

_____

_____

_____

_____

_____

_____

_____

A NOTE FROM CANDACE

Our times of brokenness are never wasted. God uses our pain and heartache to help us learn to depend on Him, understand more fully the suffering Jesus endured to save us, and develop compassion for other people who are broken and in need of our support.

Loving and Forgiving Others

LUKE 6:27–37 (NKJV)

"But I say to you who hear: Love your enemies, do good to those who hate you, bless those who curse you, and pray for those who spitefully use you. To him who strikes you on the one cheek, offer the other also. And from him who takes away your cloak, do not withhold your tunic either. Give to everyone who asks of you. And from him who takes away your goods do not ask them back. And just as you want men to do to you, you also do to them likewise.

"But if you love those who love you, what credit is that to you? For even sinners love those who love them. And if you do good to those who do good to you, what credit is that to you? For even sinners do the same. And if you lend to those from whom you hope to receive back, what credit is that to you? For even sinners lend to sinners to receive as much back. But love your enemies, do good, and lend, hoping for nothing in return; and your reward will be great, and you will be sons of the Most High. For He is kind to the unthankful and evil. Therefore be merciful, just as your Father also is merciful.

"Judge not, and you shall not be judged. Condemn not, and you shall not be condemned. Forgive, and you will be forgiven."

How would you describe someone who shows mercy to other people?

According to these verses, how does God treat unthankful and evil people? How do you tend to treat such people?

How does God want you to treat people who hate you, curse you, use you, and steal from you?

REMEMBER:
WE ARE
ALL
BROKEN
AND IN
NEED
OF
FORGIVENESS.

Think of potential "enemies" in your life—people you have a difficult time loving or forgiving. What are some practical steps you can take this week to move toward loving or forgiving those people?

_____

_____

_____

_____

_____

_____

_____

_____

_____

_____

_____

_____

_____

_____

YOUR BIGGEST TAKEAWAY

DAY 21

Living in the Light

Ephesians 5:8–20 (CEV)

You used to be like people living in the dark, but now you are people of the light because you belong to the Lord. So act like people of the light and make your light shine. Be good and honest and truthful, as you try to please the Lord. Don't take part in doing those worthless things that are done in the dark. Instead, show how wrong they are. It is disgusting even to talk about what is done in the dark. But the light will show what these things are really like. Light shows up everything, just as the Scriptures say,

> "Wake up from your sleep
>   and rise from death.
> Then Christ will shine on you."

Act like people with good sense and not like fools. These are evil times, so make every minute count. Don't be stupid. Instead, find out what the Lord wants you to do. Don't destroy yourself by getting drunk, but let the Spirit fill your life. When you meet together, sing psalms, hymns, and spiritual songs, as you praise the Lord with all your heart. Always use the name of our Lord Jesus Christ to thank God the Father for everything.

How would you describe a person who lets their "light shine"?

How should we live as "people of the light" in response to God's forgiveness of our sins and healing of our brokenness?

According to these verses, what attitudes and actions please God? What attitudes and actions should we avoid?

Make your *LIGHT* shine.

How can you live in a way this week that will shine the light of God's love on

other people so they, too, can clearly see how God heals broken people?

YOUR BIGGEST TAKEAWAY

Comforting Others

JOB 2:11–13; II CORINTHIANS 1:3–7 (ESV)

Now when Job's three friends heard of all this evil that had come upon him, they came each from his own place, Eliphaz the Temanite, Bildad the Shuhite, and Zophar the Naamathite. They made an appointment together to come to show him sympathy and comfort him. And when they saw him from a distance, they did not recognize him. And they raised their voices and wept, and they tore their robes and sprinkled dust on their heads toward heaven. And they sat with him on the ground seven days and seven nights, and no one spoke a word to him, for they saw that his suffering was very great.

Blessed be the God and Father of our Lord Jesus Christ, the Father of mercies and God of all comfort, who comforts us in all our affliction, so that we may be able to comfort those who are in any affliction, with the comfort with which we ourselves are comforted by God. For as we share abundantly in Christ's sufferings, so through Christ we share abundantly in comfort too. If we are afflicted, it is for your comfort and salvation; and if we are comforted, it is for your comfort, which you experience when you patiently endure the same sufferings that we suffer. Our hope for you is unshaken, for we know that as you share in our sufferings, you will also share in our comfort.

When in your life have you received comfort from other people during a time of sorrow or difficulty? When have you offered comfort?

How do periods of suffering in our lives help us learn how to comfort other people?

How do you think God uses suffering to bring people closer to Him and closer to one another?

COMFORT

IS MEANT TO BE

SHARED.

What are some ways you can offer comfort this week

to the people in your life who are suffering?

A NOTE FROM CANDACE

Sharing your story of how you were broken and how Jesus restored you is one of the kindest things you can do. I have experienced discrimination in the faith department for sure. But to me, it's all been worth it—chances are, my story has brought hope and comfort to people. My story is about God's love, and that's everything, isn't it?

Remaining Thankful

Psalm 30:1–5, 11–12 (NKJV)

I will extol You, O Lord, for You have lifted me up,

And have not let my foes rejoice over me.

O Lord my God, I cried out to You,

And You healed me.

O Lord, You brought my soul up from the grave;

You have kept me alive, that I should not go down to the pit.

Sing praise to the Lord, you saints of His,

And give thanks at the remembrance of His holy name.

For His anger is but for a moment,

His favor is for life;

Weeping may endure for a night,

But joy comes in the morning. . . .

You have turned for me my mourning into dancing;

You have put off my sackcloth and clothed me with gladness,

To the end that my glory may sing praise to You and not be silent.

O Lord my God, I will give thanks to You forever.

What can you thank God for today?

David, the author of this psalm, described God's anger as momentary and His favor as lasting. How does your view of God's anger and God's favor compare to David's?

How have you experienced God's healing in your life? How did you respond to that healing?

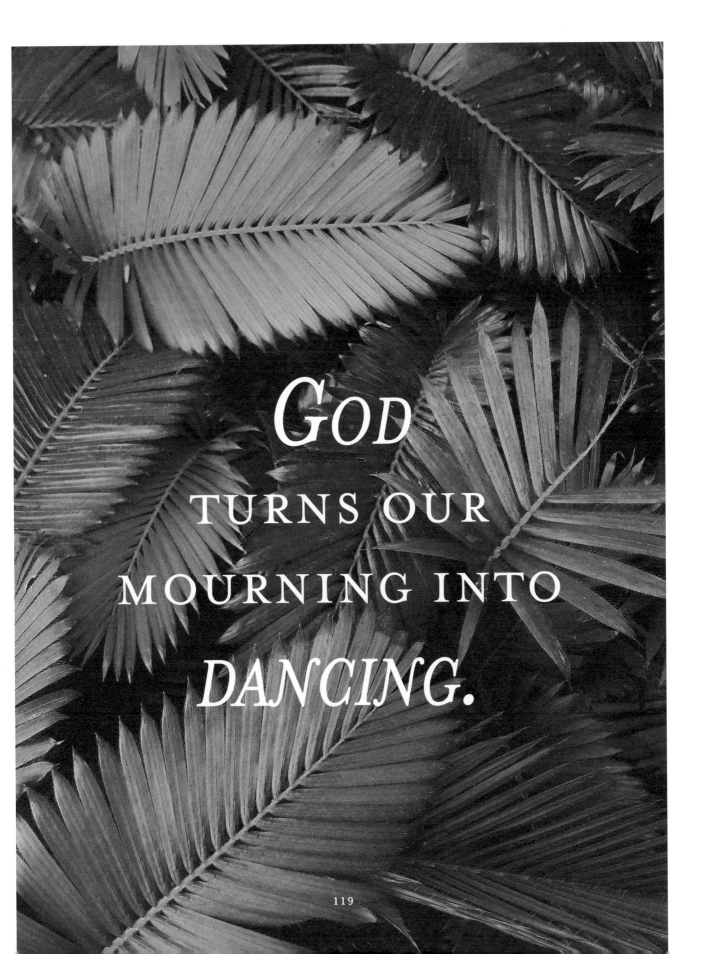

GOD TURNS OUR MOURNING INTO DANCING.

What encouragement do you receive from these verses? If you'd like, write a prayer, asking

God to give you joy and a heart of thankfulness for His work of healing in your life.

YOUR BIGGEST TAKEAWAY

Relying on Jesus

II Corinthians 12:6–10; Hebrews 4:14–16 (NIV)

Even if I should choose to boast, I would not be a fool, because I would be speaking the truth. But I refrain, so no one will think more of me than is warranted by what I do or say, or because of these surpassingly great revelations. Therefore, in order to keep me from becoming conceited, I was given a thorn in my flesh, a messenger of Satan, to torment me. Three times I pleaded with the Lord to take it away from me. But He said to me, "My grace is sufficient for you, for My power is made perfect in weakness." Therefore I will boast all the more gladly about my weaknesses, so that Christ's power may rest on me. That is why, for Christ's sake, I delight in weaknesses, in insults, in hardships, in persecutions, in difficulties. For when I am weak, then I am strong.

Therefore, since we have a great high priest who has ascended into heaven, Jesus the Son of God, let us hold firmly to the faith we profess. For we do not have a high priest who is unable to empathize with our weaknesses, but we have one who has been tempted in every way, just as we are—yet He did not sin. Let us then approach God's throne of grace with confidence, so that we may receive mercy and find grace to help us in our time of need.

What weaknesses in your character or abilities do you struggle with?

What do you think the apostle Paul meant by his words "for when I am weak, then I am strong"?

According to Hebrews 4:14–16, why is Jesus able to empathize

with us and help us in our weaknesses?

DENY YOUR *WEAKNESS,* AND YOU WILL NEVER REALIZE *GOD'S STRENGTH* IN YOU.

—JONI EARECKSON TADA

The verses from II Corinthians encourage us to rely on Jesus' power—not our own strength—for enduring the trials in our lives. What experiences have you had with leaning on yourself or leaning on Jesus during difficult times in your life?

YOUR BIGGEST TAKEAWAY

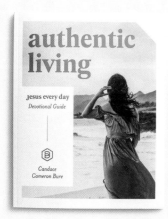

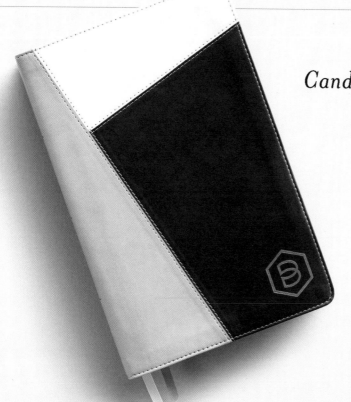